Miracles

Poems selected by Dennis Saunders
Photographs by Vincent Oliver

Evans Brothers Limited London

Miracles (an extract)

Why, who makes much of a miracle?
As to me I know of nothing else but miracles,
Whether I walk the streets of Manhattan,
Or dart my sight over the roofs of houses toward the sky,
Or wade with naked feet along the beach just in the edge of
   the water,
Or stand under trees in the woods,
Or watch honey-bees around the hive of a summer forenoon,
Or animals feeding in the fields,
Or birds, or the wonderfulness of insects in the air,
Or the wonderfulness of the sundown, or of the stars shining
   so quiet and bright,
Or the exquisite delicate thin curve of the new moon in spring;
These with the rest, one and all, are to me miracles,
The whole referring, yet each distinct and in its place.

To me every hour of the light and dark is a miracle,
Every cubic inch of space is a miracle,
Every square yard of the surface of the earth is spread with the
   same,
Every foot of the interior swarms with the same.

To me the sea is a continual miracle,
The fishes that swim—the rocks—the motion of the waves—the
   ships with men in them,
What stranger miracles are there?

Walt Whitman

Egg

Egg O egg
shape of mouth
saying O

not speaking
keeping your
secrets

    O
little world
keeping life
warm and dumb

until *crack!*
and the world
begins

    beak
pecks and wet
from within
squeaks

    a chick.

Keith Bosley

Shining things

I love all shining things—the lovely moon,
The silver stars at night, gold sun at noon.
A glowing rainbow in a stormy sky,
Or bright clouds hurrying when wind goes by.

I love the glow-worm's elf-light in the lane,
And leaves a-shining with glistening drops of rain,
The glinting wings of bees, and butterflies,
My purring pussy's green and shining eyes.

I love the street-lamps shining through the gloom,
Tall candles lighted in a shadowy room,
New-tumbled chestnuts from the chestnut tree,
And gleaming fairy bubbles blown by me.

I love the shining buttons on my coat
I love the bright beads round my mother's throat.
I love the coppery flames of red and gold,
That cheer and comfort me when I am cold.

The beauty of all shining things is yours and mine,
It was a lovely thought of God to make things shine.

Elizabeth Gould

Who?

Who made the sky?
Who made the earth?
Who thought of my or anyone's birth?

Who made the stars?
Who made the moon?
Who thought of night or morning or noon?

Who made the bees?
Who made the grass?
Who made the bonnie wee laddie and lass?

Who made the sun?
Who made the rain?
Who thought of the horse's tail and mane?

Who made the trees?
Who made them tall?
Won't somebody tell me who made it all?

Jane Cattermull

Golden glories

The buttercup is like a golden cup,
The marigold is like a golden frill,
The daisy with a golden eye looks up,
And golden spreads the flag beside the rill,
And gay and golden nods the daffodil,
The gorsey common swells a golden sea,
The cowslip hangs a head of golden tips,
And golden drops the honey which the bee
Sucks from sweet hearts of flowers, and stores and sips.

Christina Rossetti

Coral

'O sailor, come ashore,
      What have you brought for me?'
'Red coral, white coral,
      Coral from the sea.

'I did not dig it from the ground,
      Nor pluck it from the tree;
Feeble insects made it
      In the stormy sea.'

Christina Rossetti

The forest

Among the primary rocks
where the bird spirits
crack the granite seeds
and the tree statues
with their black arms
threaten the clouds,

suddenly
there comes a rumble,
as if history
were being uprooted,

the grass bristles,
boulders tremble,
the earth's surface cracks

and there grows

a mushroom,

immense as life itself,
filled with billions of cells
immense as life itself,
eternal,
watery,

appearing in this world for the first

and last time.

Miroslav Holub
translated by
Ian Milner and George Theiner

The new city

Thousands upon thousands,
Wings quivering, weaving
A tissue rustling with sound,
The joyous swarm hovers over
The honey-rich, abandoned hive.

The queen, light-blinded,
Heavy with eggs,
Settles on unaccustomed wings.
Silently, lovingly the gold-black
Undulating carpet enfolds her.

In their myriads they hang, motionless.
Peaceful, patient,
Waiting, waiting.
Waits too the straw-hatted bee-keeper
Upturned hive at hand.

Suddenly, vigorously
He shakes the laden bough.
Like over-ripe fruit
The rich cluster of bees
Fall.
A continuous gold-flecked
Stream of black cascades until
The hive is a dark, mysterious, sun-fermented pool,
From which arises a deep hum of content as
The bees rejoice.

The new city is founded.

T. H. Parker

Snowflakes

Sometime this winter if you go
To walk in soft new-falling snow
When flakes are big and come down slow

To settle on your sleeve as bright
As stars that couldn't wait for night
You won't know what you have in sight—

Another world—unless you bring
A magnifying glass. This thing
We call a snowflake is the king

Of crystals. Do you like surprise?
Examine him three times his size:
'At first you won't believe your eyes.

Stars look alike, but flakes do not:
No two the same in all the lot
That you will get in any spot

You chance to be, for every one
Come spinning through the sky has none
But his own window-wings of sun:

Joints, points, and crosses. What could make
Such lacework with no crack or break?
In billion billions, no mistake?

David McCord

Was worm

Was worm

swaddled in white
Now tiny queen
in sequin coat
peacockbright

drinks the wind
and feeds
on sweat of the leaves

Is little chinks
of mosaic floating
a scatter
of colored beads

Alighting pokes
with her new black wire
the saffron yokes

On silent hinges
openfolds her wings'
applauding hands
Weaned

from coddling white
to lakedeep air
to blue and green

Is queen

May Swenson

From the shore

A lone gray bird,
Dim-dipping, far-flying,
Alone in the shadows and grandeurs and tumults
Of night and the sea
And the stars and storms.

Out over the darkness it wavers and hovers,
Out into the gloom it swings and batters,
Out into the wind and the rain and the vast,
Out into the pit of a great black world,
Where fogs are at battle, sky-driven, sea-blown,
Love of mist and raptures of flight,
Glories of chance and hazards of death
On its eager and palpitant wings.

Out into the deep of the great dark world,
Beyond the long borders where foam and drift
Of the sundering waves are lost and gone
Of the tides that plunge and rear and crumble.

Carl Sandburg

Fueled

Fueled
by a million
man-made
wings of fire—
the rocket tore a tunnel
through the sky—
and everybody cheered.
Fueled
only by a thought from God—
the seedling
urged its way
through the thicknesses of black—
and as it pierced
the heavy ceiling of the soil—
and launched itself
up into outer space—
no
one
even
clapped.

Marcie Hans

The onion

The half onion lay on the table;
  Bitter, hated and unwanted.
The white flakes of the outer shell
  Lay scattered around.
The layers were peeling off
  In a dejected, ungainly fashion.
But underneath it was delicate and fragile.
  Thin, thin green lines,
Curving outwards from the centre.
  Thin, thin pale layers,
Each in a different shade of white,
  Curling smoothly round the outside to the top, where
A rough brown crest adorned the onion
  Where it had been wrenched from stalk.
It was an outcast.
  But to me it was
A thing of beauty.

Caroline Bisson, aged 11

New life

Through the mist a stallion bellowed,
It proclaimed the new-born foal,
Through the mist, a new, strange cry,
It echoed through my soul.

Horses live and die,
Foals are born each year,
But my pony's first cry,
Will echo ever near.

In that stable many foals,
Had uttered their first cry,
But no child had loved it,
Quite so much as I.

When the stable is in ashes,
When the foal is dead and gone,
That cry will ever echo,
Like a child's first song.

Janet Welch

who knows if the moon's

who knows if the moon's
a balloon, coming out of a keen city
in the sky—filled with pretty people?
(and if you and i should

get into it,if they
should take me and take you into their balloon,
why then
we'd go up higher with all the pretty people

than horses and steeples and clouds:
go sailing
away and away sailing into a keen
city which nobody's ever visited,where

always
        it's
            Spring) and everyone's
in love and flowers pick themselves.

                                    e. e. cummings

Acknowledgements

For permission to reproduce copyright material the
Editor and Publishers are indebted to the authors and
the following:

Angus & Robertson (UK) Ltd. for 'Egg' by Keith
Bosley from *And I Dance*; Blackie & Son Ltd. for 'The
New City' by T. H. Parker from *It Makes You Think*;
Granada Publishing Ltd. for 'who know's if the moon's
a balloon' from *The Complete Poems of e. e. cummings*
(MacGibbon & Kee) and 'The Onion' by Caroline
Bisson from *Poems From A Competition* (Blond
Educational); George G. Harrap & Co. Ltd. for
'Snowflakes' by David McCord from *Mr. Bidery's
Spidery Garden*; Harcourt Brace Jovanovich, Inc. for
'Fueled' by Marcie Hans from *Serve Me A Slice Of
Moon* and 'From the Shore' by Carl Sandburg from
Chicago Poems; Penguin Books Ltd. for 'The Forest' by
Miroslav Holub translated by George Theiner from
Selected Poems (Penguin Modern European Poets);
May Swenson for 'Was Worm' by May Swenson from
A Cage of Spines; World's Work Ltd. for 'New Life' by
Janet Welch and 'Who' by Jane Cattermull from
Elizabethan Poetry Award Competition.

Every effort has been made to trace the owners of
copyrights, but we take this opportunity of tendering
apologies to any owners whose rights may have been
unwittingly infringed.